# A Dog 'DLA' Afternoon

By Stephen Glenn Large

ISBN-10: 1545311080
ISBN-13: 978-1545311080

# CONTENTS

# SETTING THE SCENE

On 1st April 2015, Lisburn City Council annexed the sleepy civil parish of Dundonald and ended Castlereagh's long established sovereignty. There was no referendum, no polls or any sort of consultation regarding public opinion. It was an arranged marriage and one that was to enjoy no honeymoon period whatsoever. The Dundonald populace felt intimidated and resistless but just when it seemed like their hopes had been demolished, a group of renegade mercenaries rose like a phoenix from the rubble. They called themselves the Dundonald Liberation Army.

Just a few months after the hostile takeover, there had been unconfirmed reports that a rebel force was assembling within Dundonald. The area had always felt the presence of paramilitary activity, with organisations such as the C.Y.M. (Cherryhill Young Militants), the D.V.F. (Dundonald Village Florists) and the O.M.D. (Old Mill Defenders) in operation at different times.

The CYM could be considered as the forerunners to the DLA after they smuggled the first consignment of Super Soakers into the area during the early Nineties. The DVF took a no nonsense approach to the vandalizing of flower beds belonging to local residents, while the short-lived OMD disbanded over regrets they had named themselves after an Eighties new wave synth group.

In mid-September of the same year, the DLA army council released a statement through a local tabloid (the Dundonald Voyeur) which voiced their opposition to Lisburn occupation and outlined their demands. The organisation's main objectives were to end Lisburn rule in Dundonald, reunify the borough of Castlereagh and establish an independent people's republic in Dundonald. The group were said to be particularly aggrieved at Lisburn's phony claim over their beloved Ice Bowl and it was this move that propelled them into an armed struggle.

In the weeks that followed the statement, Dundonald and Lisburn were thrust into conflict as DLA water-bombs burst across the new 'super-council'. By in large, the DLA enjoyed the unwavering support of the Dundonald people but anyone who was found to be dissenting would be severely dealt with. The DLA ruled their territory with an iron rod and administered 'de-baggings' to anyone found to be engaging in anti-social behaviour or who was outspoken against their regime.

Armed with Super Soakers, the DLA waged its watery war across the new borough. However, they watched on in dismay at how their struggle was being portrayed via the media. The army council decided if they were going to win this war then they would need to fight on all fronts and therefore they required a political strategy. The D.I.C. (Dundonald Independence Committee) was established with the objective of having a legitimate political agenda running in tandem with the DLA's armed campaign.

Barry Mellon, a former DLA prisoner, was elected the DIC head and he embarked upon a series of press conferences which the Lisburn authorities dismissed as nothing more than just 'terrorist propaganda'. Lisburn Council adopted a policy of banning the voices of representatives of paramilitary groups during this time but the media found a way around the ban by dubbing Mellon's voice with that of an actor. Viewers and listeners often heard Mr Mellon's words spoken by celebrities such as Bill Cosby and Vincent Price.

However, despite the liberation movement's efforts to engage in constructive dialogue and steer away from a path of violence, no solution has been found. People on both sides of the divide have continued to see much water-shed and a resolution to the problem seems further away than ever. The name given to this etho-nationalist conflict is commonly known as 'The Difficulties'.

STEPHEN GLENN LARGE

# ACT ONE
## SCENE ONE

*Two men and a woman, all wearing a combination of sportswear and camouflage, pull crudely fashioned balaclavas over their heads. Their body dimensions are an insult to the athletic apparel that they adorn, whilst the lopsided eye-holes they have carved make their woollen masks look as though they were tailored for Sloth from 'The Goonies'. Each of them is carrying a sports grip and a fully filled Super Soaker. They burst through the doors of a local food bank.*

JOHN 'CRAZY HORSE' MCCRACKEN AKA HORSE
This is a stickin' fuck up. I mean a –

*The three renegades survey their surroundings.*

TINA 'JEBS' ANDERSON
No, it's ok. I think you were right the first time.

DAVY 'THE VENEZUELAN' TAYLOR
What is this?

HORSE
It's a food bank.

DAVY
I can see it's a food bank. But what are we doing in it?

HORSE
You said you wanted to do a local bank?

DAVY
As in one fulla money - not one fulla nappies and tins of soup!

HORSE
Well ya should've been more specific then.

DAVY
More specific? When someone suggests 'let's do a bank' what else could they possibly mean?

HORSE
Could've been a blood bank -

TINA
Are you not barred?

DAVY
How do you manage to get yourself barred from a blood bank?

TINA
The last time he tried to donate a pint of blood, he was so pissed, there was a head on it.

HORSE
Or it could've been a sperm bank?

DAVY
It feels like I'm in a sperm bank.

HORSE
Why?

DAVY
Coz I'm surrounded by wankers.

TINA
So what are we gonna do now?

BIG SADIE
Please take whatever you want, just don't hurt me.

TINA
C'mon let's just get outta here. We haven't stolen
anything. She doesn't even know our names.

HORSE
Tina's right Davy. Let's just leave.

DAVY
You fuckin' moron!

TINA
C'mon, before someone sees us and rings the peelers.

BIG SADIE
Listen to her son. It's never too late to do the right
thing.

DAVY
Who are you?

BIG SADIE
Sadie. I volunteer here.

DAVY
There must be something we could steal Sadie?

BIG SADIE
This is a non-profit, charitable organization son. We have nothing here except basic provisions and non-perishable items.

HORSE
Have you any chocolate biscuits?

DAVY
Are you havin' a fuckin laugh Horse?

HORSE
No Davy, I'm taking a wee weak turn. I forgot my insulin.

*Horse goes weak at the knees, like Bruce Grobbelaar during a penalty shootout.*

DAVY
Your insulin?

HORSE
Sure I'm diabetic now.

DAVY
Tina, go & see if you can find Horse some chocolate biscuits for Christ's sake.

*Tina exits.*

BIG SADIE
You're holding up a food bank in broad daylight. It's only a matter of time before someone phones the peelers son.

DAVY
It's only a matter of time, eh? Are you a fortune teller or
something?

BIG SADIE
Funny you should say that, I used to be a medium.

DAVY
What are you now? An extra-large?

BIG SADIE
I'll break your jaw you cheeky F'er!

*Big Sadie attempts to square up to Davy but she
has the pointed end of two Super Soakers thrust
into her face.*

BIG SADIE
Think you're hard, do ye? Pointing your pistols at an
aul doll?

HORSE
Just do as you're told love and you won't get soaked.

DAVY
Is there anyone else in here?

BIG SADIE
No it's just me.

*A loud groaning noise.*

DAVY
What the hell was that?

BIG SADIE
Eh, sorry, that was probably my stomach. I'd an Indian at
Lunchtime which hasn't agreed with me.

HORSE
I love a good Indian. What'd you have?

BIG SADIE
Some sorta green curry. I spilt some down my
blouse like a big chile.

*Horse has a closer examination.*

DAVY
Saag?

HORSE
Aye, they are a bit. But in fairness, she's well into
her 50s Davy.

*Another load groan.*

DAVY
There it is again.

HORSE
What?

DAVY
*(to Sadie)* Are you sure you're alone?

BIG SADIE
I'm positive. Now look, there's nothing here to steal so why
don't the both of you just piss away off?

*Kelly enters. She is young, attractive and heavily pregnant. She's
clutching her bump with one hand and a page in the
other.*

KELLY
Sadie I might just go home early today. I've all the
invoices finished and these pains are getting stronger
and more frequent.

*Kelly looks up and SCREAMS. She puts her hands in the air.*

BIG SADIE
I'm sorry Kelly. I thought I would've got rid of them
before you came out of that office.

KELLY
Who are you? What do you want?

BIG SADIE
Calm down love. They aren't going to hurt us.

KELLY
But they've got weapons.

BIG SADIE
Come on now. Try not to get excited. Not in your
condition.

*Kelly looks down to the floor.*

KELLY
I'm soaking.

*Davy nudges Horse.*

DAVY
See that? I've still got it kid!

BIG SADIE
Don't flatter yourself Quasimodo. You've a bake on ye like a bulldog
gargling piss.

KELLY
My waters have broken.

HORSE
Come on Davy, let's go. This is bloody mental.

DAVY
No one's going anywhere until I tell them to. I'm the
brigadier here. I give out the orders. You're only a foot soldier.

HORSE
Wha? I thought you said I was being promoted to Team
Commander?

DAVY
After this ballix? The only reason I'm not demoting
you is because no lower rank exists!

HORSE
I guess that means no pay rise now either? There goes
the fuckin' conservatory.

KELLY
Please, I'm pregnant. I'm a week overdue. I could go
into labour any minute.

BIG SADIE
Please, let her go.

DAVY
No one's going anywhere until I say.

BIG SADIE
Put yourself in her husband's shoes lads. How would you
feel if your wife was pregnant and being held
hostage?

HORSE
That could never happen to me love. I went and got
myself sorted out - if you know what I mean? *(winks)*

DAVY
You got the snip? You kept that quiet. Was it
sore?

HORSE
Oh aye, pure achin' so it was. I got it done a couple of months ago. I
wasn't able to drive home or anything.

DAVY
Doctors' orders?

HORSE
No I parked in a disabled spot and got fuckin' clamped.
I had to walk it back.

DAVY
Jaysus.

*DAVY winces.*

KELLY
Please, just let us go. Me and my husband have been
trying for years to have children. We've spent
thousands of pounds trying to get pregnant.

HORSE
Did yous go for that there UVF treatment love?

SADIE
IVF?

HORSE
No need to bring politics into this now love. So was it
expensive?

DAVY
What the fuck does it matter?

HORSE
Was just askin' like.

KELLY
Please, just leave us alone.

*Sirens and flashing blue lights.*

DAVY
There's the peelers! How'd they even know we were here? *(to Sadie)*
Did you warn them? Did you trip the alarm?

SADIE
There is no bloody alarm. I guess we figured that no
one would ever be low enough OR stupid enough to rob a food
bank, so we didn't get one.

HORSE
Well I guess you underestimated the DLA then, didn't
you?

SADIE
DLA? Hold on a minute. Are 'yous' the Dundonald
Liberation Army?

DAVY
Aye.

BIG SADIE
I thought you boys were supposed to protect the locals?

DAVY
We do.

BIG SADIE
By robbing a charity which provides food and
toiletries to the most impoverished members of the
community?

DAVY
We were supposed to rob a real bank. But our German
friend, Einstein over there, got the wrong intel.

KELLY
He's Austrian.

HORSE
No love. You must be thinking about
Crocodile Dundee or something.

*Davy walks over to Kelly and Sadie*

DAVY
You two, get into that office. Things could get ugly.

SADIE
Things got ugly in here the minute you two walked in.

DAVY
Shut up and get in there.

*Kelly and Sadie exit. Horse walks across the stage
as though he's just received a prostate
examination by Freddie Kruger and stops at a
window. This walk continues throughout.*

DAVY
Why are you walkin' like you've shit yourself? You've
been mincing about like a big girl's blouse the whole
day.

HORSE
I read somewhere that a banana a day keeps your colon
clean. So I had one every day for a month.

DAVY
So why are you waddling?

HORSE
I only found out yesterday you were supposed to eat them.

DAVY
Have a look out that windy. What do you see?

HORSE
We're surrounded boss. I haven't seen this many peelers since Dunkin Doughnuts had that closing down sale.

DAVY
Do you recognise any of them?

HORSE
Na, I don't think so.

DAVY
Who's in charge?

HORSE
A big lad. He looks like a Brazilian.

DAVY
South American?

HORSE
A big baldy twat.

*Tina enters.*

TINA
I found these Hobnobs out the back. The place is like a maze.

*Horse grabs the biscuits and eats one like an animal.*

DAVY
We've got company.

*Tina peers through the window.*

TINA
The peelers! How'd they know we were here?

DAVY
God knows.

TINA
Should we squirt our way out boss?

DAVY
That'd be suicide. They could have a water canon or
anything out there for all we know.

TINA
There's BRU TV Live out there too.

HORSE
My teachers always said I'd amount to nothing but here I am, on the
news.

DAVY
Turn that TV on.

*Light on News Reporter.*

NEWS REPORTER
Good afternoon and welcome to BRU TV Live. We bring you
this special news bulletin live from outside the Manna
Food Bank in Dundonald Village. A short while ago,
three members of the Dundonald Liberation Army broke
into this local food bank behind us. They are believed
to be armed with Super Soakers and water bombs. Police
were alerted to the break in when one of the DLA
operatives tagged the three suspects in a Facebook post
which read: Just robbin' the ballix clean outta this
bank with the lawds... yeeoo... Uppa DLA'. The reasons
for the siege have not yet been established - but that

won't stop us wildly speculating! PSNI Castlereagh were unavailable for comment but are said to be treating the situation as ridiculous.

# ACT ONE
## SCENE TWO

*Davy is pointing his Super Soaker at Horse and Tina.*

DAVY
Which one of you dopey bastards checked us in on
Facebook? *(Pointing at Tina)* Was it you?

TINA
No boss. I swear.

DAVY
Prove it.

*Tina produces a mobile phone.*

TINA
It couldn't have been me. I've no data left - I accidentally
downloaded a picture of Stephen Nolan.

DAVY
It was you *(Pointing at Horse)*. I should drench you for
this insubordination.

HORSE
I'm sorry Davy.

DAVY
Fuckin' tout!

TINA
Take it easy Davy. Horse is thicker than an MLA's wallet but he's no tout. He's always doing stupid stuff like this! Like remember that time he got drunk and started posting pictures of his dick?

DAVY
On Facebook?

TINA
No, through his neighbour's letterbox.

*Sadie enters.*

BIG SADIE
Have you seen the news?

*Davy removes his balaclava.*

DAVY
Aye.

TINA
Davy, what are ya doing takin' your mask off?

DAVY
Thanks to him, wearing this balaclava is about as pointless as a dwarf's yoyo!

HORSE
I'm sweltered in mine.

TINA
Same here. My top lip's wetter than the
front row of a Michael Buble concert.

DAVY
Take them off then.

*Tina removes her balaclava. Horse doesn't.*

HORSE
I don't want to reveal my true identity. I wish to
remain anonymous.

BIG SADIE
Remain anonymous? You've only been in here five minutes
and we already know your nickname; you're type one
diabetic and you've had the bloody snip!

*A peeler's voice can be heard via a megaphone.*

OFFICER GOODFELLOW (V/O)
This is Constable Goodfellow of the PSNI. We have you
completely surrounded. Come out with your hands up -
and a packet of custard creams please.

HORSE
I don't wanna go back to jail Davy. They only have
Playstation 3s in there.

DAVY
No one's going back to jail ya header. Tell them we
have taken three prisoners - and we'll drench them if
we have to.

TINA
Three?

DAVY
Aye, well your woman's pregnant.

SADIE
Taking a foetus hostage. Disgraceful.

*Horse leans out the window.*

HORSE
We have a trio in here.

OFFICER GOODFELLOW (V/O)
That's awfully kind of you but we're gonna stick with
the custard creams.

DAVY
They're still talking about biscuits the dopey fuckers.
Tell them we've got hostages Horse!

HORSE
We've got hostages. One of them is pregnant - and we'll
drench them unless our demands are met.

OFFICER GOODFELLOW (V/O)
Take it easy in there. What are your demands?

HORSE
What are our demands Davy? *(whispering)*

DAVY
Fuck knows?

HORSE
F -

DAVY
Shut up you! Maybe we could buy ourselves some time
here with some dummy demands. Tell them, we
will read out a list of our demands, shortly.

HORSE
We shall read announce our demands shortly.

OFFICER GOODFELLOW (V/O)
Very well. Could you give us a status update on the
custard creams?

DAVY
Close that windy on the them gluebegs!

*Horse closes the window.*

DAVY
Is there another way out of here except through that
front door *(to Sadie)*?

BIG SADIE
This place used to be a post office. There's an old
passageway that leads you out to the back of the
building.

DAVY
Happy days! Horse, you and me are gonna make up some bogus
demands. Hopefully that'll keep the peelers occupied. Tina, I want
you up the back passage.

*Tina exits.*

SADIE
What about our Kelly?

HORSE
Awk, he's alright but his last album was shite.

SADIE
*OUR KELLY*, my niece, as in the heavily pregnant young
woman in the next room about to give birth?

DAVY
Once we find a way out of here, you're both free to go.

SADIE
And what if you don't find a way out of here any time
soon?

DAVY
We'll cross that bridge when we get to it.

SADIE
But she's about to pop any minute!

DAVY
We'll deliver it ourselves if we have to but I am not about to
surrender our bargaining chip.

HORSE
Me a deliver a baby? I couldn't even pass that first
aid course at tech Davy!

DAVY
Really?

HORSE
They said I couldn't do the QPR properly.

SADIE
CPR?

HORSE
Nah, I'm a Liverpool man love.

*Load groans. Kelly enters.*

BIG SADIE
Don't worry Kelly, you'll be in the hospital soon.
Isn't that right lads?

DAVY
Trust me. The last thing I wanna witness is
another birth. I'm still having flashbacks from seeing

my daughter's.

HORSE
They tell you to stay away from the business end, don't
they though?

DAVY
That's a myth! No matter where you stand, you see
plenty of business.

HORSE
Really?

DAVY
Trust me. Any man who says watching the birth of their
child is the greatest experience of his life is a
fucking liar. Watching that baby's giant head smash its
way through your favourite place in the world *(gets
emotional)*. It's like watching Stephen Nolan try on
your favourite jumper.

*Kelly moans loudly. Sadie is rubbing her back.*

KELLY
I can't believe this is happening to me. It's a living
nightmare.

BIG SADIE
Awk come on now, I'm sure it could be worse.

KELLY
Worse? How could it possibly be any worse than this? I
wanted it to be special. Something I'd remember for the
rest of my life.

BIG SADIE
In fairness, giving birth in a food bank while being
held hostage isn't something you'll be likely to forget
in a hurry. No matter how much counselling you get.

*Kelly starts to cry.*

DAVY
Take her back into that office and calm her down. Me
and Horse need to come up with these dummy demands to
keep the peelers off our backs!

BIG SADIE
Come on love.

*Sadie and Kelly exit.*

DAVY
Right, what will we tell these pigs we want?

HORSE
Insulin.

DAVY
We can't ask for that.

HORSE
Why?

DAVY
Cos then they'll know we have a weakness and they'll
play on it.

HORSE
But Davy, I could end up in a coma. I could even end up
brain damaged.

DAVY
It's a risk I'm willing to take.

HORSE
Fair enough. Just get me a bottle of Lucozade and a
Bounty then.

DAVY
Fine. What else?

HORSE
What about a signed Northern Ireland shirt?

DAVY
Not a bad idea. We could hang that up in the Shebeen.

HORSE
Ask them to get Carl Frampton, Rory McIlroy and Michael
O'Neill to sign it.

DAVY
We could stick it on eBay and make a few bob.

HORSE
Aye!

DAVY
What else?

HORSE
What about a couple of bottles of Buckfast?

DAVY
Excellent big man. Every great paramilitary operation
in history has been born out of tonic wine. These demands
should keep those black bastards occupied while we find
a way outta here.

*Tina enters.*

TINA
The back passage is blocked up. It had a Lisburn City
Council logo on the brick work.

DAVY
The bastards. Did you find anything else?

TINA
There's a staircase which leads to the roof.

DAVY
Did you find another way out of here?

TINA
There's no way out of here - except through that front
door.

DAVY
Get me the big girl.

*Light on News Reporter.*

NEWS REPORTER
There have been further developments in the DLA food
bank robbery. It is believed that as many as three
hostages are being held inside the building. So who are
these people behind the masks? Our sources say:

*Light on Davy*

Davy 'The Venezuelan' Taylor - Reputed top man of the
DLA. The origins of his nickname 'The Venezuelan' are
unclear, although his aunt does own a solarium in
Dundonald. He ordered the water-bombing of Lisburn City
Council offices earlier this year.

*Light on Horse*

John 'Crazy Horse' McCracken - Hates Lisburn with a
passion after breaking his leg during a football match
against Ballymacash Hard Men Seconds. He completed two
full months of an art diploma at Bangor Tech and was
immediately placed in charge of murals and other spray

paint related vandalising.

## *Light on Tina*

And Tina 'Jebs' Anderson - Founder member of the DLA's sister organisation Vicious Action Against Jugs (VAAJ). This vigilante group dish out severe punishments such as de-baggings, diddy-nips and Chinese burns to anyone found guilty of anti-social behaviour and jug dealing. Although rumour has it that Tina sells jugs herself.

# ACT ONE
## SCENE THREE

*Outside the food bank. Davy is with Sadie.*
*He has a pistol to her head. They are face-to-face with the police.*
*We hear a helicopter track.*

DAVY
Helicopters? I might end up getting a mural out
of this.

BIG SADIE
I'm delighted for you and your legacy. Gabshite.

DAVY
Now I'm warning you lot *(to police)*. No funny business or I'm
soaking her on the spot.

OFFICER GOODFELLOW
No tricks.

BIG SADIE
I hope you're working on a plan officer. My niece is in
labour in there.

OFFICER GOODFELLOW
I can assure you we're doing everything possible to
bring an end to this situation. How are you being
treated? Are you feeling any
empathy towards your captors?

BIG SADIE
What do ya mean?

OFFICER GOODFELLOW
Sometimes the victims of hostage-taking can develop
feelings of trust or affection towards their captors ?

BIG SADIE
This ball-bag? I wouldn't pish on him if he were on fire.

DAVY
You tell those pigs to keep their distance. They're
getting too close. Anything happens to me, Horse and
Tina are in the back with the girl -

OFFICER GOODFELLOW
I understand.

*Goodfellow signals to stand down.*

OFFICER GOODFELLOW
Come on Davy. Quit while you're ahead. All you've got
here is attempted robbery.

BIG SADIE
Attempted armed robbery.

DAVY
Shut you up!

OFFICER GOODFELLOW
OK, armed robbery. No one's been soaked. No one is
going to worry about the kidnapping charges. You'll get

five years, you could be out in a year. We have your
usual cell ready. There's a Playstation 4 in it now
Davy.

DAVY
Nice try Goodfella.

OFFICER GOODFELLOW
Goodfellow.

DAVY
You's have me on armed robbery and
kidnapping. If I give up, I'm going down quicker than a
hard-on in Susan Boyle's bedroom.

OFFICER GOODFELLOW
What is it you want Davy? Have you got your demands?

*Enter Officer Ursula Bonnet. She takes out a
notepad.*

DAVY
We, the Dundonald Liberation Army, demand the
following: A bottle of Lucozade Original and a Bounty;
a Northern Ireland football jersey signed by Carl
Frampton, Rory McIroy and Michael O'Neill. And two
large bottles of Buckfast Tonic Wine.

OFFICER GOODFELLOW
Is that it *(laughs)*?

DAVY
Eh, no. Of course that's not it. That's just for
starters.

OFFICER GOODFELLOW
Did you get all that Officer Bonnet?

OFFICER BONNET
Yes sir.

OFFICER GOODFELLOW
Give me the list. I shall call in these 'demands'.

*Officer Goodfellow turns away and talks into the radio on his lapel.*

DAVY
Well hello there officer *(to Bonnet)*. May I say you're looking well this afternoon.

OFFICER BONNET
You may not.

BIG SADIE
I hope to F' that's another Super Soaker poking me in the back Davy.

DAVY
Bonnet? That's an unusual surname.

OFFICER BONNET
My grandfather was French.

DAVY
Do you know who is sexy as fuck and speaks French?

*Officer Bonnet gives a disinterested shrug.*

OFFICER BONNET
Who?

DAVY
Moi.

SADIE
Oh give me a bucket.

DAVY
Allow me to introduce myself. David Taylor. 'Tap mawn'
of the Dundonald Liberation Army and proud winner of
brigadier of the year 2017.

OFFICER BONNET
Don't worry Mr Taylor, you really need no introduction.

DAVY
So you're familiar with my work?

OFFICER BONNET
Let's just say your reputation precedes you.

DAVY
My reputation? The women used to throw themselves at me, you
know? They said I looked like your man off the TV with the
moustache.

SADIE
One of the Chuckle Brothers?

DAVY
Tom Selleck ya cheeky cow. Do you know what the lads
nicknamed me back then?

SADIE
Enlighten us.

DAVY
Polyfiller.

SADIE
Polyfiller?

DAVY
Because I filled so many cracks.

SADIE
Or maybe it's because most of the women were plastered.

OFFICER GOODFELLOW
We managed to fulfil all your demands -

DAVY
Great —

*Officer Goodfellow hands Sadie a bag. Davy peeks inside.*

DAVY
There's my Bucky!

OFFICER GOODFELLOW
- Except one.

DAVY
What's that?

OFFICER GOODFELLOW
Both Carl Frampton and Michael O'Neill signed your Northern Ireland top.

DAVY
And what about McIlroy?

OFFICER GOODFELLOW
I'm afraid not. He refused to travel to Dundonald. He heard that the place has been infected with the Zika Virus.

DAVY
That's Horse's fault.

SADIE
How come?

DAVY
Look at all the size of
his wee head. He's probably scared him off.

OFFICER GOODFELLOW
You got what you wanted Davy - now what about releasing the
hostages?

DAVY
Once I release them, what's to stop you bastards coming
in here and drenching us?

OFFICER GOODFELLOW
No one's going to get drenched Davy, you have my word.

DAVY
Once I get safely back inside, I will release ONE hostage.

SADIE
Release our Kelly.

OFFICER GOODFELLOW
The rapper?

SADIE
Jaysus Christ! I'm surrounded by imbeciles. Kelly, my
niece. You know, the one who's pregnant and about to go
into full blown labour?

DAVY
We need an ambulance.

OFFICER GOODFELLOW
Fine. I'll arrange that now.

DAVY
Good. Once it arrives, she can go. You have my word.

OFFICER GOODFELLOW
And then?

DAVY
Then you await our next set of demands.

SADIE
Oh wonderful. I get to spend the next few hours in
there with these head-the-balls until they decide what
they want from the Chinese.

DAVY
We're going back inside. Don't try anything now.

OFFICER GOODFELLOW
Trust me Davy. You have my word that nothing will
happen without your knowledge.

DAVY
My da always told me to never trust a peeler but I've a
good feeling about the rapport we're building Goodlad.

OFFICER GOODFELLOW
Goodfellow.

DAVY
Whatever.

*Davy disappears back inside the food bank along
with Sadie.*

NEWS REPORTER
Welcome back to BRU TV Live. We're still here outside
the Manna Food Bank in Dundonald Village, where just
moments ago, reputed top man of the DLA, Davy 'The
Venezuelan' Taylor, emerged from the building holding a
hostage at gunpoint. We are told that the brigadier
made a list of demands which included a Bounty and some
tonic wine.

We're joined by concerned resident Des McShitstir, who actually lives outside of Dundonald but wades into these types of debates to whip up tension. So Des, tell us what happened to you here today?

## DES MCSHITSTIR
I was just going to the local shap to get my wee granny a loaf of bread and a battle of milk when I heard there was a tense hostage situation developing here. So I decided to take an unnecessarily long route to the shops via the food bank and was denied access by the PSNI. A person should be able to go about their normal daily lives which might involve a lot of unnecessary trips to the shop - without being subjected to such brutality.

## NEWS REPORTER
There you have it folks. A frail old woman has been denied the opportunity to drink some milk because of the actions of these so-called freedom fighters. Are these the actions of defenders of the community? This reporter doesn't think so.

# ACT ONE
## SCENE FOUR

BIG SADIE
An ambulance will be here soon Kelly. Just hold on
love.

DAVY
Did any of yous see that woman peeler out there by the
way? *(peeking out the window)* She can put me in cuffs
any day!

BIG SADIE
You're such a male chauvinist.

DAVY
What's that mean?

BIG SADIE
It means you don't like women.

DAVY
Are you trying to say that I'm some sort of fruit or
something?

TINA
I think it's more to do with you being a sexist big bastard Davy.

DAVY
Hold on, that's not true. I respect women. Like just this morning,
when I saw a woman driving the Ballybeen bus, I smiled. It reminded
me about how far we'd come as a
society and it made me proud.

BIG SADIE
Awk really?

DAVY
Aye. Then I waited on the next bus *(laughs)*.

BIG SADIE
It's men like you that give your entire gender a bad
reputation.

DAVY
What do ya mean?

BIG SADIE
You've about as much admiration and respect for women
as a Saudi Arabian gangster rapper. The both of you are
a disgrace to men everywhere.

HORSE
Hold on! What'd I do?

BIG SADIE
Sure didn't you turn the taps off at the sperm
factory before your wife could experience the joys
of motherhood - ya selfish big prick?

HORSE
No!

BIG SADIE
Yes!

HORSE
I didn't!

BIG SADIE
You should be ashamed of yourself!

HORSE
I didn't get the snip - I'm infertile!

*Gasps*

HORSE
I only said I got the chop because I was embarrassed. I thought if people found out, they wouldn't be afraid of me anymore.

DAVY
Are you trying to tell me my right-hand man's been firing more blanks than a starter's pistol?

BIG SADIE
I'm sorry love. I didn't mean to out you this way.

HORSE
It's ok, you weren't to know. I haven't told anyone else about it.

TINA
That's a shame Horse. I know how keen you were to have a wee family of your own. Have you considered going down the foster route?

HORSE
If I do turn to drink, it won't be that cheap Australian piss.

TINA
No, I mean would you raise a child that has been placed into care?

HORSE
I dunno. I haven't really thought about it.

BIG SADIE
There are lots of young children out there crying out
for a wee mammy and daddy.

HORSE
Do you get to pick one or is it like a lucky dip?

BIG SADIE
I'm not really familiar with the process. Why?

HORSE
It's just that, what if… what if the chile's da was
a… you know, a Lisburnian?

*The three DLA gang spit on the floor.*

BIG SADIE
Awk don't be so ridiculous. All babies are born the
same. It's how they're brought up that moulds them into
the adults they become.

HORSE
So it's my da's fault I am the way I am. Is that what
you're saying?

BIG SADIE
Well, sorta.

HORSE
Coz he went to jail when I was wee and then I ended up
in jail a couple of years ago.

BIG SADIE
For what?

HORSE
Actual bodily harm. I was behind the missus in the queue in
Homebase. She was holding a big shelf and whenever she got to the
till the fella asked her, 'Are you gonna put that up
yourself love?'.

BIG SADIE
So?

HORSE
So I floored him with one dig and said 'No it's going
in the dining room ya pervert'.

BIG SADIE
Awk, you really love your wife, in your own mental way.

HORSE
When you're willing to do six months in The Labyrinth
Prison for her, you know she's the one.

TINA
Do you know when I knew our Winkie thought I was 'the
one'?

BIG SADIE
How?

TINA
He started wearing condoms with other women.

BIG SADIE
Jaysus!

TINA
I wish our relationship was more like yours Horse.

HORSE
My wife gives me a kiss every morning as soon as I open
my eyes.

BIG SADIE
Do you kiss her back?

HORSE
No, on the mouth usually.

TINA
So are you going to keep trying for a baby?

HORSE
That's why I was asking Kelly about that UVF treatment.

BIG SADIE
IVF

HORSE
Look, I said earlier to stop the political talk!

BIG SADIE
It's very expensive son.

HORSE
I know that and that's why I jumped at the chance to be
involved in this robbery. I was going to use my share
of the money to pay for another course of UVF
treatment.

TINA
IVF

HORSE
What is wrong with you people? I'm spilling my guts
here and all 'yous' can think about are paramilitaries.

BIG SADIE
So what about all this talk of using the money to help
liberate Dundonald?

HORSE
Awk that's a lot of aul ballix so it is.

*Davy raises his Super Soaker and points it at Horse.*

DAVY
I should soak you to the skin for that sort of talk.
It's treason!

HORSE
Awk wind yer neck in Davy. A free Dundonald is just a
pipe dream now. People have seen too much water-shed.
Most of them are actually happy enough being a part of
Lisburn Council now.

DAVY
I'm warning you Horse. You stop this nonsense or I'll
drench ye on the spot.

HORSE
Go ahead. I'm fed up with it all so I am. I only joined
up cos I didn't want that job in IKEA. To tell you the
truth, I even went up to use Lagan Valley LeisurePlex
and it was far better than the Ice Bowl.

*Davy's heard enough. He lunges at Horse and a
grappling match ensues. In the resulting chaos,
both men drop their water pistols, one of which is
picked up by Big Sadie. She breaks up the scuffle
by dispersing a few squirts of water in the air,
then points the pistol at both men. Tina then
points her pistol at Sadie and a stand-off ensues.*

TINA
Come on now big girl. Put the water pistol down before
somebody gets soaked.

BIG SADIE

Your two mates will be drenched before you even get a
squirt off - and less of the big girl. You aren't
exactly Twiggy yourself.

TINA

It would appear that we've reached a bit of an impasse.

BIG SADIE

It would indeed.

TINA

So what now?

DAVY

Just soak the aul bat. So what if she squirts us first?
I'd rather be drenched than go back to The Labyrinth
anyway. The cause is more important than freedom - or
life!

TINA

I'm sorry Davy but I've got something in common with
Horse.

HORSE

You've a low sperm count too?

TINA

I've been having my doubts about the cause.

DAVY

What doubts?

TINA

Not just about the cause Davy. About everything. I've
devoted too much time to the DLA and my life is falling
apart around me.

DAVY
What are you on about ya header?

TINA
While I'm out at nights trying to liberate Dundonald,
my husband's out trying to impregnate most of it.

DAVY
Has Winky got another bit on the side?

TINA
He blames me because I'm out at nights and he gets
'lonely'.

HORSE
If he gets lonely he should borrow some of my porn, I've a
mountain of it at home.

DAVY
Most wankers do.

HORSE
The specialist at the clinic suggested me & the Mrs
watch it together. You know, to get us in the mood.
I've some magazines there too if you want them. They're
all brilliant - but stay away from that new Northern
Irish one called 'barely legal'.

DAVY
How come?

HORSE
The centrefold was just two gay men
eating a wedding cake. What a let-down.

TINA
He'd ride a cracked plate that husband of mine. Did you
hear he even slept with that hooker with the one arm?

DAVY
Wee Wendy One-Wing? You're joking me?

HORSE
If she's only got one arm, can you still catch
the clap off her?

BIG SADIE
Jaysus Christ the night!

TINA
So, I've been feeling really down about it all. I even
booked an appointment with the doctor. Do you know what
he said?

*They all shrug or shake their heads.*

TINA
He said that I might be bipolar.

BIG SADIE
How'd you feel about that?

TINA
I didn't know whether to laugh or cry.

BIG SADIE
Did you ask him for a second opinion?

TINA
Aye he said I was ugly too.

DAVY
So what if Winkie's been doin' more riding than Tony
McCoy. That's no excuse to be doubting the cause!

HORSE
Tell him about your Emma as well.

DAVY
What about wee Emma?

HORSE
She's on the drugs.

DAVY
Wee Emma's on drugs?

TINA
She's not on the drugs!

HORSE
I thought you said she loved crack?

TINA
No I said she's a lesbian.

DAVY
Wee Emma's a vage-tarian?

TINA
You see? I know this sort of thing is frowned upon in
our organisation - unless you're in jail, then it's like Mardi Gras.
But I thought that if it got out, I'd be
de-bagged - or even drenched.

BIG SADIE
You've a lot on your plate love. No wonder you've been
feeling down lately.

TINA
I was thinking of getting out of here for a while.
Maybe a fresh start somewhere else?

BIG SADIE
Well what's stoppin' ya?

TINA

Well I'm currently embroiled in a tense hostage situation. But before this ballix, I was gonna use my share of the money to bugger off and take the family on a cruise. You know, try to get things resolved.

HORSE

And are you sure you're not firing blanks? It'd be great to have someone to talk to like.

TINA

Positive Horse.

HORSE

What about you Davey? Is your sperm lethargic?

DAVY

I'm fine in that department Horse. I've sperm like little versions of Michael Phelps.

HORSE

Aye, well I remember you in school. You'd ballix like little Duncan Goodhew's until you were about 16.

DAVY

I was a late bloomer.

TINA

Everyone thought you were a girl in first year.

HORSE

It didn't help that your middle name was Courtney. A girl's name.

DAVY

I was named after my uncle Courtney, actually..

*Laughter.*

DAVY

Laugh all you want but my uncle Courtney slept with dozens of women.

BIG SADIE

Was he good looking?

DAVY

No he was a sex offender.

TINA

Remember when we were sixteen you always used to get turned away by the bouncers?

DAVY

That's because I had the physique of a 6-year-old Romanian gymnast. What didn't help matters was that I was always stood beside Horse. He hit puberty about p5 and by the time he was sixteen he was hairier than Robin Williams.

HORSE

There was one wee bar in Newtownards though that always served you. What was it called?

DAVY

The Toby Jug. It fronted as an aul man's pub but it had a back room that could only be described as a glorified crèche. It was filled with prepubescent children in Henry Lloyd jumpers.

TINA

It was a complete shite-hole.

DAVY

Aye but when you have a ballbag like Kojak's elbow and you're built like a Kenyan runner, it was also the best nightclub in the world.

HORSE
My da wouldn't let me drink in Ards. He said they all
buck their cousins.

DAVY
Sure did your da not buck his cousin?

HORSE
Don't you bring my ma into this!

DAVY
School, the best days of your life they say. I hated
every second of it. The kids got away with murder back
in those days. Even in primary school.

TINA
In fairness to the primary school kids, most of them
were blocked on Top Deck.

DAVY
It's crying shame that.

TINA
What?

DAVY
Unless the shops bring back shandy drinks and sweetie
cigarettes, the next generation of school kids might
never experience the joy that accompanies a life of
alcohol dependency and respiratory illness.

HORSE
Ah, those were the days. Standin' in the playground,
neckin' Shandy Bass while watchin' two stray Labradors
ride the life clean outta each other.

*A loud groan stops the trip down
memory lane. Sadie is torn between her freedom and*

*helping Kelly. After a short deliberation she*
*drops her weapon.*

BIG SADIE
You two children can squabble until you're heart's
content. There's a young girl in there that needs my
help.

*Sadie walks towards office door.*

TINA
Wait!

*Sadie stops in her tracks and puts her arms in the*
*air.*

TINA
I'll help you.

BIG SADIE
Come with me love. You're the nearest thing to a gynaecologist in
here anyway!

TINA
How'd you figure that one out?

BIG SADIE
You're used to working with fannies *(points over*
*her shoulder at Davy and Horse)*.

*Tina sets down her pistol and follows Sadie. Horse*
*and Davy crawl across the floor and pick up the*
*weapons.*

# ACT ONE
## SCENE FIVE

*Davy and Horse are alone inside the food bank.*

OFFICER GOODFELLOW (V/O)
This is officer Goodfellow. Are you ready to make your
proper demands?

DAVY
Shit! The demands! Suggestions?

HORSE
Woah! Don't ask me, I just paint the murals and do the
odd baitin' if we're a man down.

DAVY
Anything at all?

HORSE
I know nothing about our ideology. I'm no Groucho Marx!

DAVY
You mean Karl Marx?

HORSE
I'm no comedian either mate.

*Davy grabs a pen and paper from a desk and starts writing.*

DAVY
Ok, what about this one. We, the Dundonald Liberation
Army, demand a public declaration by Lisburn City
Council that it is the right of all the people of
Dundonald, to decide the future of Dundonald - so it
is.

HORSE
Smashin' mate.

DAVY
Thank you.

HORSE
Anymore like that?

DAVY
What about this one - we demand a declaration of intent
to withdraw any claim that Lisburn has over our beloved
Ice Bowl.

HORSE
Brilliant. What else?

DAVY
And underage drinking in The Moat Park will become
compulsory and will recommence immediately.

HORSE
About time too. Since they banned drinking in public
places, the park has lost its fear factor at night
times.

DAVY
Some of the best nights of our lives were spent

drinking in that Moat Park. Remember standing at the
footbridge, tankin' five tins of Royal Dutch and a
bottle of Old E? Wee girls comin' up to ye and asking
'hey wee lad, will you see my mate?'. If you played
your cards right, your fingers
smelt like they'd worked their way through a multi-pack
of Scampi Fries at the end of the night.

HORSE
Those were the days Davy. Kids nowadays. They're too
busy wasting their time at school - but life's real
education happened at that bridge! Do you know many
fourteen-year-olds nowadays that could hold two
battered sausages with one hand while fair-diggin'
someone from Tullycarnet with the other?

DAVY
Here - speaking of which, did you hear about the fella
who got his ballix knocked in in The Moat Park last
night?

HORSE
No?

DAVY
Good. I warned him to keep his mouth shut.

HORSE
What else Davy?

DAVY
The Park and Ride terminal. We demand that it be
renamed.

HORSE
Why?

DAVY
It sounds like a doggin' spot or somethin'.

HORSE
I was gonna go doggin' once but didn't.

DAVY
Great story.

HORSE
I'd no licence at the time. My ma wouldn't give me a lift.

*Sadie enters. Loud groans can be heard coming from the office.*

BIG SADIE
The baby is on its way.

*Davy looks at his watch.*

DAVY
Could she hold it in for another five minutes? We're almost finished the demands.

BIG SADIE
Hold it in? It's not a shite! Never mind your demands! You need to get an ambulance here now!

DAVY
Horse, go out there and tell them there's a girl about to drop a baby in here. We need an ambulance.

*Horse exits.*

BIG SADIE
Just keep breathing love.

*Kelly groans amusingly.*

DAVY
She isn't half making a meal of it.

BIG SADIE
Excuse me?

DAVY
I'm sure it's sore and all but it's not as if she stood on a plug or
something.

BIG SADIE
There's baby trying to force its way out of
her vagina. It's going to sting a little.

DAVY
Well it couldn't be that sore.

BIG SADIE
And how do you figure that one out? Bearing in mind you
wouldn't have the medical background to squeeze a spot!

DAVY
A kick in the ballix - now
that's real pain. Women will have lots of children but
you never hear a man ask for a second or third boot in
the spuds, do you?

BIG SADIE
If anyone deserved multiple kicks in the spuds it's
you!

*Horse re-enters.*

HORSE
The peeler says they rang an ambulance ages ago.

BIG SADIE
Well where the hell is it?

HORSE
He said it's stuck in a queue of traffic because of a

broken down bus. According to the radio it's a mile long.

BIG SADIE
That's a fuckin' disgrace.

HORSE
Anno that's what I said - buses that length shouldn't be allowed on the roads.

*Kelly moans in agony. The contractions are becoming more intense. Birth is imminent.*

BIG SADIE
It's no use. We can't hold on any longer. We're going to have to deliver this baby ourselves. Quick Horse, get me some hot towels.

HORSE
Do you really think we have enough time to shave her?

BIG SADIE
It's not for shaving, it's to prevent infection you glue bag! Start looking!

*Horse exits.*

BIG SADIE
It's like some ridiculous parody movie - Three DLA men and a baby.

OFFICER GOODFELLOW (V/O)
This is Officer Goodfellow. The ambulance has arrived. Requesting permission to enter the building.

BIG SADIE
Let him in son. We need to get this girl to a hospital.

*Davy approaches the door.*

DAVY
Come in *(shouts)*.

*Officer Goodfellow enters. His hands are in the
air.*

OFFICER GOODFELLOW
I'm completely unarmed.

DAVY
Well you won't mind if I have a little check. Just to
be sure?

OFFICER GOODFELLOW
Go ahead.

*Davy carries out a very thorough search.*

DAVY
OK. You're clean.

BIG SADIE
Clean? I didn't know whether you were frisking him or
checking his prostate.

OFFICER GOODFELLOW
Where's the girl?

BIG SADIE
She's in there. Will I fetch her?

*Davy nods. Sadie exits.*

OFFICER GOODFELLOW
We're going to take her now Davy. Just like we agreed.
Do you have your new demands ready?

DAVY
I have them written down.

*Davy hands the written list to Goodfellow who
quickly scans them.*

OFFICER GOODFELLOW
These are a little more ambitious Davy. These are going
take time to arrange.

DAVY
We have all the time in the world Goodguy.

OFFICER GOODFELLOW
Goodfellow.

DAVY
Whatever.

*Kelly and Sadie enter. Kelly lets out another
groan. It's the loudest yet.*

DAVY
That definitely sounded like the most painful one so
far. Are you crowning?

KELLY
When this is over I'm going repeatedly prove your
theory correct.

DAVY
What theory?

KELLY
That a kick in the balls IS more painful than child
birth.

*Sadie escorts Kelly over towards Officer*

*Goodfellow.*

OFFICER GOODFELLOW
It's never too late to end this entire thing and walk
out that front door with me Davy.

DAVY
Never.

OFFICER GOODFELLOW
Davy this could be your last chance.
I can't stress enough - this may be
your last chance.

DAVY
Goodbye Goodlad.

OFFICER GOODFELLOW
Goodfellow.

DAVY
Whatever.

*Goodfellow and Kelly exit through the front door.
Davy locks it behind them.*

SADIE
You should've taken the opportunity to end this son. I
get the feeling he was trying to warn you about
something there.

DAVY
Nonsense. There are two things about me love. One, is
that I have a great knack for reading people and two,
is that I'm an excellent judge of character.

SADIE
Is that why you picked Horse to run the intel for this
hugely successful operation?

*Horse enters.*

HORSE
Right. I've got the towels. Where is she?

*Sadie gives Davy a knowing look.*

*Tina enters.*

TINA
Quick. They're making a move to get in.

DAVY
What?

TINA
I could see from the roof. They're preparing to storm
the place.

BIG SADIE
Nostradamus strikes again.

DAVY
Well you didn't see it coming either, Mrs 'I
used to be a medium'.

*There are bangs as if somebody is trying to burst
through the front door.*

DAVY
You're a double-crossin' bastard Goodchap!

TINA
Quick, bring Sadie and get onto the roof. The steps are
just across the hall. We'll block the stairwell with
crates full of grub!

*The banging gets louder.*

DAVY
Come on let's go!

SADIE
On the roof? I can't deal with heights.

DAVY
Is it vertigo?

HORSE
No sure Tina said it was only across the hall.

*The banging gets worse.*

HORSE
I think I'm taking a another wee weak turn.

DAVY
Don't you go fainting on me you big pansy!

*Horse collapses but Davy catches him before he
hits the ground.*

DAVY
Let's go!

*The DLA and Sadie hastily exit.*

# ACT TWO
## SCENE ONE

NEWS REPORTER
And this just in... following an unsuccessful attempt
by the PSNI to storm the building, the DLA have taken
their remaining hostage onto the roof.
In an attempt to diffuse the situation, the PSNI have
drafted in Dundonald Independence Committee (DIC) chief
Barry Mellon. Mellon, a former DLA prisoner and now the
head of the DLA's political wing, has arrived on the
scene from DIC Headquarters just moments ago...

*Barry Mellon is stood outside the bank clutching a*
*megaphone. Tina and Davy are on the roof.*

TINA
How's Horse doing?

DAVY
Sadie's trying to bring him round with a bottle of Lucozade
over there.

BARRY MELLON

This is your elected representative speaking. Not only would I like to engage in constructive dialogue with all parties involved here today - but I would also like to take this opportunity to appeal for calm amongst young Dundonaldians - despite this latest example of blatant Lisburn and PSNI discrimination.

TINA

Is that Barry?

DAVY

Aye. Down there playing to the cameras as usual.

BARRY MELLON

I would call upon my comrades on top of the food bank to enter into dialogue as soon as possible?

DAVY

Barry you've more faces than the Albert Clock.

TINA

And every one of them ugly as fuck.

BARRY

It's time to surrender comrades.

DAVY

Fuck off Barry. The DIC no longer represents the DLA. We do not believe that an independent republic of Dundonald can be brought about by political means only.

BARRY MELLON

There has been enough watershed Davy. The DLA army council has already committed to peace and a political agenda. If you go against the army council you will splinter the movement and can no longer be members of the DLA.

DAVY
See if we care ya bearded ballix ye. We've already
decided to form our own organisation.

TINA
Have we?

BARRY MELLON
What do you call yourselves then?

DAVY
Hold on a minute. Right, what are we calling ourselves?

TINA
What about the Ballybeen Reaction Unit?

DAVY
The BRU? We can't have the BRU and the DLA.

TINA
You know how serious we are about jug dealin'? What
about Vicious Action Against Jugs.

DAVY
The VAAJ?

*Sadie emerges.*

BIG SADIE
You can't call yourselves that for F's sake.

TINA
Why not?

BIG SADIE
You can't be running about shoutin' UPPA VAAJ.

DAVY

She's right. Just think about the recruitment days. 'If anyone would like to be in the VAAJ just put your hand up?' Half them young ones won't know whether we're asking them to join up or if we're giving them a license to finger all round them.

TINA

Why not just keep it nice and simple? We wish to remain true to the original principles of the DLA whilst continuing our armed struggle against Lisburn tyranny. Let's call ourselves DLA for Life?

DAVY

I like it. Now what about a slogan? Something that encapsulates entire ideology as well as the situation we currently find ourselves in?

TINA

What about 'No Surrender'?

DAVY

Na. It'll never catch on. What about, 'Never don't give up'?

TINA

Does that even make sense?

DAVY

It's totally DLA - I mean DLA for Life.

*Davy turns to Barry.*

DAVY

From this day forth, we shall be known as 'DLA for Life'. Never don't give up!

BARRY MELLON
This is tantamount to treason Davy. Wait until the army
council hears about this - not that I'll be the one to
tell them of course! I don't know who they are. I was
never in the DLA *(winks at the audience)*.

DAVY
Away back up to your wee cushy number on the hill
Barry. Leave the freedom fighting to us real men.

BARRY MELLON
Ah well. Back to crackin' jokes on Twitter for me.

*Barry exits.*

TINA
What are we gonna do now Davy? We've fractured the
whole movement.

DAVY
I haven't a clue to be honest. I never thought this far
ahead.

*Enter Special United States Peace Envoy, Buzz
Jackson.*

US PEACE ENVOY
Could I talk to 'The Venezuelan' please?

TINA
Who's the big Yank?

DAVY
No idea.

US PEACE ENVOY
Could I speak to David Taylor?

DAVY
You're talking to him!

US PEACE ENVOY
Hi. Buzz Jackson, Special United States Peace Envoy.

DAVY
What's happenin' big lad?

US PEACE ENVOY
It looks as though you guys need some help?

DAVY
Aye, you could say that.

US PEACE ENVOY
We hear you guys have been on the lookout for a new
flamboyant lunatic to support your cause, ever since we
took out Colonel Gaddafi for not sharing his oil?

DAVY
Aye! Big Gaddafi used to send us shipments of Super
Soakers during the early years of our campaign!

US PEACE ENVOY
Oh yeah? And what'd he get out of this arrangement?

DAVY
We used to send him some second hand fancy dress
costumes left over from DLA fundraisers. He used to
wear them at conferences across the globe.

US PEACE ENVOY
Well I think I have a suitable replacement for you!

DAVY
Oh aye? Who's that then?

US PEACE ENVOY
President Donald Trump.

DAVY
Trump?

US PEACE ENVOY
He promised the American people that he'd turn every US
state into a Muslim-free gun range and now he wants to
help the beleaguered people of Dundonald.

DAVY
Is that your man with the wild hair?

US PEACE ENVOY
The very guy!

DAVY
What does Donald Trump want with us?

US PEACE ENVOY
Mr President was hoping to build a hotel and casino in the
Castlereagh area.

DAVY
A casino *(scoffs)*. Good luck getting that one past the
DUP.

US PEACE ENVOY
But this televised hostage situation is generating a
lot of negative publicity and scaring off potential
investors.

DAVY
So?

US PEACE ENVOY
So he was hoping we could resolve this matter by
offering you guys a few 'incentives'.

DAVY
We're listening.

US PEACE ENVOY
Donald has promised to build a wall around Castlereagh
to keep out Lisburnians, as well as any other smelly
refugees.

DAVY
Really?

US PEACE ENVOY
He's also promising free sunbeds and a life-time supply
of tanning injections, for all the inhabitants of
Dundonald.

DAVY
Wow. That'll save the boys a fortune on St Tropez *(fake
tan)*.

US PEACE ENVOY
Wonderful isn't it?

DAVY
You know, I think Donald would fit right in here in
Belfast to be fair. He's intolerant of other religions
and he loves building walls.

US PEACE ENVOY
Yeah and we've also noticed it's socially acceptable in East
Belfast for ruthless tyrants to have blonde highlights.

DAVY
I think we may have a deal my American buddy!

US PEACE ENVOY
Although, there are a few provisos -

DAVY
There's always a catch.

US PEACE ENVOY
In exchange for financial aid in assisting the
Dundonald Liberation movement, we will require the
following -

DAVY
Here we go.

US PEACE ENVOY
Your town must change its name to Dun-Donald Trump with
immediate effect.

DAVY
Fair enough.

US PEACE ENVOY
As a mark of respect, every Sunday, all inhabitants
must wear ill-fitting strawberry blonde toupees.

DAVY
Not a problem.

US PEACE ENVOY
And finally. As a personal favour to Donald, he would
like you DLA guys to water-bomb all local burrito bars
that might employ any of those light brown
people.

DAVY
Now hold on just a minute. There's one thing you should
know about us Belfast folk. We might be a wee bit
racist - but we're only racist when it suits us. A
staple Belfast diet comprises of at least ten to twelve
take-away meals per week. If we start water-bombing the
burrito bars and the Indians, who's gonna make our
grub? Our mothers? Our wives? Fuck that!

US PEACE ENVOY
Mr Taylor -

DAVY
You tell that Oompa Loompa lookin' wig-wearin' moron,
to take his hotel, his casino and his tanning
injections, and stick them up his hole, because the DLA
does not discriminate whether it's those smelly brown people,
useless old people or even whinging women. The only people we
discriminate against are the Lisburnians - and we do it
with pride! Now piss off back to Washington.

*The Peace Envoy exits.*

# ACT TWO
## SCENE TWO

NEWS REPORTER

The stand-off continues here outside the Manna Food Bank after failed negotiations involving local and international delegates. As we swiftly approach tea time, the PSNI are becoming more agitated.

SADIE

I tried giving Horse some sugary drinks but it's not working.

TINA

We need to get him some insulin Davy.

DAVY

Even his pancreas is fuckin' useless.

SADIE

Seriously son, if we don't get his blood sugars sorted. He'll die.

DAVY

We all knew about the risks of this mission before we agreed to do it. If he dies, he'll do so in the line of duty. He'll be a hero. He might even get a mural out of it.

TINA

Really? And who's gonna paint it? Sure Horse is the one who did the art course at Bangor Tech.

DAVY

You're right. I suppose I have no choice. We'll have to get someone else to paint it!

TINA

You can't be serious Davy. Horse has a wife. He's our friend.

DAVY

That big wanker lying over there is the reason we're in this mess to begin with. Me and you are looking at prison - or even a soaking - because of his stupidity.

SADIE

Is your cause so important to you son that you're willing to let your mate die?

DAVY

Yes.

TINA

I'm asking the peelers for help.

DAVY

I'm the brigadier here and you will follow orders or -

TINA

Or what Davy? Soak me if you have to. But I'm not going to stand by and watch OUR friend die.

*Tina peers takes a tissue from her pocket and draws a red cross on it. She hangs it over the building.*

OFFICER GOODFELLOW
Who is injured? Has the hostage been harmed? Let us speak to the
hostage.

BIG SADIE
I've a chronic case of cauliflower ear from listening
to the shite that's been talked up here - but apart
from that I'm fine.

OFFICER GOODFELLOW
Then who is in need of medical assistance?

TINA
It's Horse. He needs insulin. He's diabetic.

OFFICER GOODFELLOW
Let me see what I can do.

TINA
Hurry, I don't know how much time he has left.

BIG SADIE
You did the right thing love.

DAVY
Bravo 'Dr Quinn Medicine Woman'. Now they have us by
the plums.

TINA
What do you mean?

DAVY
They know that Horse is running out of time and they're
going to use it as leverage against us.

BIG SADIE
They aren't going to risk a man's life son.

### DAVY
Did you come up the Lagan in a bubble? The peelers are worse than us. They'll give us an ultimatum. Surrender or he dies.

### TINA
It's time to start being realistic Davy. The peelers have us surrounded. We're stuck on this roof. Horse is dying. What option do we have other than surrender?

### DAVY
We still have her *(pointing his gun at Sadie)*. While we have a hostage, I'm still running this show.

### BIG SADIE
You've taken it as far as you can. It's time to count your losses. The longer this goes on, the more trouble you're getting into.

### OFFICER GOODFELLOW
We have acquired the insulin.

### TINA
Oh thank you. Quickly, throw it up here.

### OFFICER GOODFELLOW
You will receive the insulin on one condition.

### DAVY
Told you!

### OFFICER GOODFELLOW
We will give you the medicine in exchange for the hostage.

*Davy grabs Sadie and puts the Super Soaker to her head.*

DAVY

And I have a different proposal for you. You have two
minutes to get that insulin up here or the big girl
gets drenched.

BIG SADIE

Come on now son. Don't be making any hasty decisions.

TINA

Davy -

DAVY

Where's your loyalty lie Tina? To the cause? To me? To
Horse? Or to this stranger? You want me to save Horse's
life - well it's her or him. You decide.

*Tina ponders this momentarily before reluctantly
raising her pistol at Sadie.*

TINA

I'm sorry Sadie.

BIG SADIE

Don't worry love. I understand.

DAVY

Two minutes officer Goodboy.

OFFICER GOODFELLOW

Goodfellow.

DAVY

Whatever. I'm going to check on Horse.

*Davy goes over to tend to Horse out of sight.*

TINA

I'm sorry Sadie. I'm sorry for all of this.

BIG SADIE
It's not your fault.

TINA
What a bloody mess. I don't know if any of us will get
out of this alive.

BIG SADIE
No matter what happens today, I'm ready to face my
maker.

TINA
You've still plenty to live for -

BIG SADIE
Have I? No kids of my own, my husband's dead. At least
I'll get to see him again if nothing else.

TINA
What was his name?

BIG SADIE
Alfie.

TINA
What was he like?

TINA
Loving, kind, generous - and VERY good in the
Bedroom department.

TINA
He was good at sex?

BIG SADIE
No, he worked for Starplan for twenty five years. He
was absolutely hopeless when it came to fanny.

TINA

Sadie *(laughs)*! That' awful you!

BIG SADIE

It's true love. Hung like a budgie's tongue he was.

TINA

*Laughs.*

BIG SADIE

Ugly as sin as well. I remember our dog, Patch. He used to close his eyes when he was humping his leg.

TINA

You say your late husband, what happened to him in the end?

BIG SADIE

He was killed by a Double Decker.

TINA

The bus?

BIG SADIE

No the chocolate bar. I'd did try to warn him it may contain traces of nuts but he didn't listen.

TINA

You're still young enough to find someone else.

BIG SADIE

I'm hitting 60 love. I'm too old for all that caper now. Besides, I've got my hands full caring for my ma.

TINA

What age is she?

BIG SADIE

In her early 80s. She's practically bed-bound now. A

full-time job it is. You wanna try living with that auld cow.

TINA
Why, what does she do?

BIG SADIE
My fuckin' head in, most of the time.

TINA
*Laughs.*

BIG SADIE
Nothing's ever good enough for her. All I do is run about like a blue arse fly after her and I don't get as much as a thank you. I come here just to get my head showered if truth be told.

*Davy rejoins them.*

DAVY
Look, no hard feelings Sadie. It's not personal.

BIG SADIE
You've changed your tune. A minute ago you were willing to let him slip into a coma.

DAVY
I should never have put him in this position in the first place. Asking Horse to organise a bank job? He still has a Henry Super Savers account.

TINA
He'd a tough upbringing dear love him.

DAVY
Aye he did. His nickname in school was 'flour'.

BIG SADIE
Flour?

DAVY
Cos he was self-raising.

TINA
His mother was a bit of a girl and was never in.

DAVY
And his da spent seven years inside.

BIG SADIE
Jail?

TINA
Agoraphobia. Never left the house.

*Davy peers over the side of the building.*

DAVY
Right Goodman *(shouting)*, your two minutes are up. I'm
gonna count to three and then I'm soaking the big girl.
ONE - TWO -

OFFICER GOODFELLOW
Stop! Ok. We'll give you the insulin. Just put the
pistol down.

*Officer Goodfellow throws up the medical pack.*

BIG SADIE
Cutting it a bit fine there lads. I was beginning to get
a complex up here.

*Tina picks up the medical pack.*

## TINA
Quickly. We've no time to lose.

*Davy, Sadie and Tina run as the lights fade.*

# ACT TWO
## SCENE THREE

*Tina is nursing Horse. Sadie and Davy are stood over him.*

TINA
How are you feeling?

HORSE
I saw the light Tina. I was beckoned by a childlike being toward a blinding light. Then my whole life flashed before my eyes. I think I was dying. Or have I died? Is this the afterlife? Am I dead?

DAVY
Dead fuckin' annoying.

BIG SADIE
Maybe you were just dreaming son. Maybe it was all that talk about your childhood and growing up?

TINA
It's funny, talking about school earlier got me reminiscing a bit about the old days too.

DAVY

School. Best days of your life they say. Absolute
shite. I hated every minute of it.

TINA

That's because you used to get picked on somethin'
shockin' Davy.

DAVY

I'd usually come home with a fat lip or a black eye.
Every day the school bully would offer me a 'fair dig'
with him and five of his mates.

BIG SADIE

Is that how you lost those teeth Davy? In a fair dig?

DAVY

Sorta.

BIG SADIE

Sorta how?

DAVY

Well if you ever come home with lipstick on your collar
and the Mrs asks how it got there. Never say you used
your shirt to wipe your dick.

BIG SADIE

Sounds to me like you got off lightly ya gabshite.
You're all the same. There's only one type of woman who
knows where her husband is all the time.

TINA

What's that now?

BIG SADIE

A widow.

TINA
So how did the beatings stop Davy?

DAVY
I just stopped going to school and went on the beak.
Then I left school with no qualifications.

HORSE
It wasn't just the bullies you'd to worry about though.
The teachers dished out more baitins than anyone. I
remember minding my own business and the next thing a
high heel hit me on the head.

BIG SADIE
Did the teacher throw it at you?

HORSE
No it was still attached to her foot.

DAVY
Did you hear about Mr Walters? It turns out he was a
paedo. Got caught with stuff on his computer.

TINA
Horse, wasn't he your form teacher?

HORSE
He never touched me!

DAVY
I'm not surprised. You were an ugly wee shite. When
you walked past Mr Walters he ate his own sweets.

TINA
Funny, huh?

HORSE
What?

TINA
One minute you're taking the register, the next you're
on one.

HORSE
I suppose it was worse in your day Sadie?

BIG SADIE
Oh aye. My teacher used to beat me on a daily basis.
For nothing most of the time.

TINA
Did you go on the beak?

BIG SADIE
I couldn't. I was home schooled by my mother.

DAVY
The whole experience scarred me beyond belief. When I
left school I was determined not be pushed around
anymore. That's when I decided I was gonna do one of
two things; join the police or the DLA.

BIG SADIE
What made you choose the DLA over the peelers?

DAVY
Both careers paid well but the DLA's hours were better.

*They all nod in agreement.*

DAVY
I remember when we all joined up together. It seemed
like the start of a wonderful journey. I joined because
there was a sense of belonging; a sense of direction -

HORSE
I thought you said you joined because you were fuckin'
Skint?

DAVY

Aye that too - but somewhere along the line the struggle against Lisburn rule became less about liberation and ideology and more about organized crime and money.

BIG SADIE

So why has it taken so long to come to this realisation son?

DAVY

I suppose I just didn't want to admit to myself that it's all been a giant waste of time. That I've devoted my time to a baseless lie.

TINA

Come on Davy. Let's just hand ourselves in. We'll be out in a couple of years and we can leave all this crap behind.

DAVY

I can't go back to prison - I can't leave Crystal behind.

BIG SADIE

Who's Crystal?

TINA

Who's Crystal Davy?

DAVY

My new girlfriend.

BIG SADIE

So there is a woman on the planet you like after all?

TINA

I didn't know you were seeing someone?

DAVY
After my marriage went down the shitter, I thought I
was destined to be a bachelor for the rest of my days. But I've
finally met someone -

TINA
So where'd you meet her?

DAVY
In the local bar.

TINA
And what does she do?

DAVY
She's a cabaret dancer.

TINA
A dancer? I bet she's got some figure.

DAVY
Oh she's something else.

HORSE
A lovely lady.

TINA
Oh have you met her?

HORSE
Aye. Davy brought her down the bar the other week. I
got chatting to her briefly in the toilets.

BIG SADIE
What were you doing in the women's toilets?

HORSE
I wasn't.

TINA
Well you must've been.

HORSE
It was definitely the men's.

TINA
How can you be so sure?

HORSE
Cos I was standing beside her having a pish.

*Everyone except Davy and Horse gasp. The penny finally drops from a great height and Horse gasps too.*

HORSE
What's goin' on Davy?

DAVY
You know Crystal. Well, she used to be, you know -

HORSE
What?

DAVY
You know (starts pointing to his crotch).

HORSE
A dick?

DAVY
A man.

HORSE
Jaysus Christ Davy. What are you sayin'? That Crystal's a fella?

DAVY
Used to be a fella.

HORSE
So does that make you - a fruit?

DAVY
You say that again and I'll soak ye.

HORSE
Well I'm very confused Davy.

BIG SADIE
So's Davy by the sounds of it.

TINA
When you say she's a cabaret dancer Davy, in which
show?

DAVY
The Lady Boys of Bangkok.

TINA
Crystal is one of the Lady Boys?

DAVY
Aye.

HORSE
You ARE a fruit!

DAVY
Look, just because I'm having sex with a Thai dancer
who used to be a man doesn't mean I'm gay.

HORSE
Well what does it mean?

DAVY

Look, let me explain. The Lady Boys had a couple of
shows in Belfast. They'd been rehearsing in the
Stormont Hotel and it was her night off. She ended up
in The Moat bar. She was sat there all alone and I
offered to buy her a drink. She spoke pretty good
English and we just hit it off right away. It was
getting towards last orders and she whispered in my ear
that she hadn't had the cock for a month. So we got a
taxi straight to The Stormont.

HORSE
And?

DAVY
Little did I know she
meant it'd been thirty days since she'd had her penis
removed.

HORSE
Why didn't you just leave?

DAVY
By the time I found out I was past the point of no
return.

HORSE
You were riding her?

DAVY
No I'd spent a fortune on drinks.

BIG SADIE
In for a penny, in for a pound, eh?

TINA
So all this time you've been giving us a hard time about our personal lives affecting our loyalty to the cause - and all the while you've been playin' hide the sausage with one of the Ladyboys of Bangkok?

DAVY
I think I love her.

HORSE
Jaysus Christ! I need a drink.

BIG SADIE
It's a food bank. Not an F'n Wetherspoons you're holding up.

DAVY
I'm still the same person I was. I haven't changed. But the heart wants what the heart wants.

HORSE
Alright Celine - just stay around the front where I can see you!

DAVY
Well since it's all out in the open, I might as well tell you all what I was going to do with my share of the money.

HORSE
Buy a house near Union Street?

DAVY
I was going to pay for the rest of Crystal's surgery. So that we could finally spend our lives together as a man and a woman.

TINA
Are you trying to tell me that you dragged us into a
failed bank robbery - which has now developed into a
hostage situation; that we're all facing jail time and
a potential drenching; just so you could have sex with
your Thai boyfriend without his balls getting in the
road?

DAVY
Technically, yes.

*Sadie laughs hysterically.*

BIG SADIE
This has to be the best thing I've ever heard. Three
big hard paramilitaries have taken me hostage so that
they can pay for a sex change, a Caribbean cruise and a
course of fuckin' 'UVF' treatment? I should drench you
all myself, never mind the peelers.

DAVY
That's why I don't wanna give up here. If this
gets out, I'll be fucked in prison.

HORSE
Happy days says you.

TINA
This is an absolute disaster!

BIG SADIE
Perhaps you all could make the best out of a bad
situation?

TINA
How can anything good come from this?

BIG SADIE
Well, like you say, you will most likely be going to

prison and your little secrets will
come out too -

## DAVY
And this is supposed to be making us feel better how?

## BIG SADIE
All I'm saying is, if the worst is going to happen then
don't let it be in vain.

## HORSE
Spit the bricks out Sadie.

## BIG SADIE
Why don't you change your demands to the three things
that you REALLY want? At least that way, even if you do
go to prison, well at least you'll have achieved your
objectives?

## DAVY
And what if they say no?

## BIG SADIE
Well then you'll be no worse off. You'll still go to
prison. But if they say yes, well then at least you'll
go to prison safe in the knowledge that the ones you
care about will be taken care of. All of this won't be in vain.

## TINA
It's worth a shot Davy. Like Sadie said, what have we
to lose now?

## DAVY
Horse?

## HORSE
Ok, I'll do it - but under one condition.

## DAVY
If we go to prison - I am not sharing a cell with you
ya big girl's blouse.

# ACT TWO
## SCENE FOUR

NEWS REPORTER
Welcome back folks.
We've just been informed that despite the fact that
only one hostage has been released from the food bank
so far, eighty-four emotional distress claims have been
submitted by people claiming to have been inside the
building. We've also been told that some relatives and loved ones
of the DLA have been ferried in by the PSNI who are
looking a speedy resolution to the situation as it gets
dangerously near to their tea break.

HORSE
Quick. Look!

*They all look over the roof.*

HORSE
Never mind the peelers. We're in deep shit now.

BIG SADIE
Why? Who is it?

HORSE
There's our Suzie! I can see your Winky too Tina.

TINA
Does he look ragin'?

HORSE
Not half as ragin' as Davy's ma looks.

DAVY
My ma's out there?

HORSE
Aye she's standing there beside Crystal.

DAVY
Crystal? I haven't told my ma about Crystal yet.

BIG SADIE
You have to talk to them.

TINA
I'll go first. Our Winky's usually in the bar at this time. I don't wanna eat into Happy Hour.

HORSE
I'll go too. I have to explain myself to Suzie. She deserves that much before I get put away.

*Horse and Tina go to the other side of the stage where a light shines on them.*

TINA
Winky.

WINKY
Tina, I thought you said you were going to the bank this morning about a loan? A fresh start you said.

TINA

In fairness now Winky, I did think we were going to the
bank earlier.

WINKY

Aye, but you neglected to mention you were going to rob
it.

TINA

Well the good news is, we didn't.

WINKY

No, you just took a pregnant woman and an old lady
hostage instead.

TINA

But I did it for us! For the family.

WINKY

So this was a romantic gesture?

TINA

Aye sort of.

WINKY

I'd have been happy with a case of beer and a blow job.
Instead, what do I get? A televised hostage situation.

TINA

And what have you ever given me? Apart from that
aggressive yeast infection?

WINKY

I apologised about that! I even went in and bought
the cream when you said you were too embarrassed to
ask.

SADIE

Who said romance was dead?

WINKY
Look, I know I haven't been a good husband -

TINA
Or a father to our Emma.

WINKY
We'll get to that! But I can't change what I've done.
I'm ashamed of myself for what I've put you through.
But I want you to know, when I was sleeping with those
other women I was thinking of you the whole time - and
it wasn't just to stop me ejaculating too quickly.

*Tina gasps.*

WINKY
Sorry. Look I'm terrible with words. I wish there was some other
way I could communicate to you both how truly sorry I am but I
can't.

TINA
Maybe with me going away for a while it will give us
time to revaluate things.

WINKY
Perhaps.

TINA
Just promise me you'll sit down with Emma and tell her
we'll support her no matter what life choices she
makes.

WINKY
I will. I'm sorry that you think I was a terrible
father.

TINA
You were a terrible father. The way you made Emma feel when
she came out...

WINKY
OK, I was a terrible father, you're right. And I'm
sorry Emma thought I was ashamed of her because she was
gay. I wasn't ashamed of her. I was just worried about
how people round here would react towards her because I
know how cruel and narrow-minded some people can be.
Because I know how cruel and narrow-minded I was. Everyone
deserves the same love and respect they had before they built up
the courage to reveal their true identity.

TINA
It's just sad that it had to reach this point before we
realised the error of our ways.

WINKY
I'm sorry love.

TINA
I'm sorry too.

*Lights go off momentarily. Switch to Horse and
Suzie.*

SUZIE
John? Are you there?

HORSE
Yes Suzie, I'm here love.

SUZIE
I heard what you tried to do John.

HORSE
I know, I'm so ashamed of myself. If you hated me and
wanted nothing to do with me I would completely
understand.

SUZIE

It's not what you did but why you did it. It was
idiotic, ill-advised and destined for failure -
that's just who you are. But you did it so we could
fulfil our dream of bringing a little baby into this
world and I could never hate you for that.

HORSE

Exactly love, that UVF treatment isn't cheap.

SUZIE

IVF

HORSE

Awk not you as well?

SUZIE

What do you mean love?

HORSE

Have you been radicalised since I've been in here?

SUZIE

John what are you on about?

HORSE

It's just that every time I've brought up our fertility
problems today everyone's immediately switched the
subject to paramilitary groups.

SUZIE

I think you're getting confused honey. IVF, it stands
for In Vitro Fertilisation -

HORSE

Are you trying to tell me I've been ringin' round all
these clinics asking how much it would cost to get the
UVF to inseminate my wife? No wonder half of them hung
up and rest threatened to phone the peelers.

SUZIE
Don't beat yourself up.

HORSE
I'm such a dick!

SUZIE
Oh come on John, you've been known to make the odd cock
up in your time. Like remember last Pan Cake Day? I
asked you to nip to the shop to get me stuff for the
crepes and you came home with a box of Immodium. Or
when I asked you to get something for cleaning windows
and you came with Norton Anti-Virus.

HORSE
And today, with this bloody Food Bank.

SUZIE
You see. It's just you, being you. There's really no
need to be so hard on yourself.

HORSE
Hold on - one of those clinics actually gave me quote!

SUZIE
Oh John, I'm going to miss you.

HORSE
I wrote you a poem my darling. To let you know how
sorry I am and how much I love you.

SUZIE
I'd love to hear it.

HORSE
Ok, here goes:
My dearest Suzie
I knew your love for me was long-term

When the clinic said I'd lethargic sperm
And even though I was firing blanks
You said you'd marry me big girl, thanks
You even gave me the full ok
When I said I was joining the DLA
We tied the knot in Bratislava
You wore white and I wore my balaclava
And now I must go away for a while
But I only wanted for us to have a chile
Fear not my love it may still be possible
I'll get my solicitor to ask for a conjugal
We'll be together again so please don't gurn
Uppa DLA and fuck Lisburn
The end.

## NEWS REPORTER
One of the relatives belongs to reputed top man, Davy
Taylor. Mr Taylor's mother, Iris, was recently
investigated for fraudulent compensation claims. Davy
Taylor has been rammed from behind by his mother's
Nissan Micra fourteen times since 2002. While Iris has
also submitted twelve separate compensation claims for
neck injuries during this period and is now referred to
by local solicitors as 'Madame Whiplash'.

## IRIS
Davy. Can you hear me?

## DAVY
Mammy

## IRIS
Don't mammy me ya wee ballix ye. What the hell are you
playing at? Get down off that roof now!!

## DAVY
It's ok ma. I've got things under control.

IRIS

Really? Because from down here it looks as though
you've made a complete ballix of things.

DAVY

I don't want you getting worried now.

IRIS

Worried? I'm not worried. I'm pure scundered. You're
letting us all down a bucket full. We're the talk of
the place.

DAVY

Where's my da?

IRIS

He couldn't face coming down here.

DAVY

Is he ashamed of me?

IRIS

No he's dyin' with a hangover. He says he might see how
he feels after his fry but if he doesn't make it down
he says he'll hopefully get up to see you in jail at
some stage.

DAVY

He couldn't be bothered basically.

IRIS

You know him son. Laziness walks in his family.

DAVY

Ma I've got somethin' to tell you.

IRIS

What is it?

DAVY
I'm in love.

IRIS
In love? I didn't even know you were seeing anyone?
Then again, I never see you these days. You never have
time for your mammy anymore.

DAVY
I met someone a few months ago. The most amazing
wonderful person.

IRIS
What's she do? This 'amazing' woman that stops you from
coming to visit your wee mammy?

DAVY
She's a dancer.

IRIS
A bloody stripper I bet.

DAVY
No mammy. A cabaret dancer.

IRIS
Really? Oh I love the cabaret shows! Maybe we could both go
together to watch her in action?

DAVY
Sure.

IRIS
Oh great! I can't wait to meet her now!

DAVY
She's moved to Dundonald to be with me. She's living
here now.

IRIS
She's here? Why haven't I met her yet?

DAVY
She's standing right behind you mum.

IRIS
Where son? I can see F' all past this big Chinese
fella.

DAVY
Ma, that's Crystal.

IRIS
Move Crystal. I can't see Davy's new girlfriend.

DAVY
Ma, Crystal is my new girlfriend.

CRYSTAL
I wait long time to meet you Mrs Iris *(deep Asian voice)*.

*Iris faints.*

DAVY
Crystal darling. Please forgive me. I did this for you.

CRYSTAL
No one ever done anything so sweet for me in all my
life.

DAVY
I might be going away for a while. I'm not sure for how
long but I've left you some ribs in the freezer. Will
you promise me darling that you'll wait for me.

CRYSTAL
I promise

DAVY
Don't cry my love.

CRYSTAL
I have tear in my eye and a lump in my throat which is
not just apple of Adam. But I have happy heart because
I know I will see you soon.

DAVY
Farewell my love!

CRYSTAL
Bye bye Davy Taylor.

## ACT TWO
## SCENE FIVE

NEWS REPORTER
Welcome back folks.
In another amazing twist, the Dundonald Liberation Army
changed their demands and requested: a Caribbean
cruise; a sex-change operation and a course of UVF
treatment - whatever that is? The police saw these
bogus demands as the final insult and offered the DLA
one thing and one thing only - unconditional surrender.

*Davy sits with his head in his hands totally
despondent.*

DAVY
The peelers thought we were raking.

TINA
The irony.

DAVY
What?

TINA
When we gave them dummy demands they thought we were
being serious and now that we've told them what we
really want they think we're joking.

106

BIG SADIE
In fairness, if someone had told you they were holding
hostages in exchange for a penis removal, would you
have believed them?

HORSE
I still can't fuckin' believe it.

DAVY
It's all been for nothing.

TINA
What has?

DAVY
All of it. This bank job. Joining the DLA. My whole
life.

BIG SADIE
It can't all have been a waste of time. Surely?

TINA
We did have some successes I suppose.

DAVY
Name me one.

TINA
What about that time we rang the doorbell on the
Lisburn Council headquarters and ran away without being
caught?

DAVY
True.

HORSE
Remember the look on those civil servant's faces?

DAVY
Aye they were raging! They had to cut their tea break
short after thirty-seven minutes.

HORSE
Or what about the time we planted those water bombs in
Lisburn City centre?

DAVY
They had to send out that disposal team
to carry out a controlled bursting.

TINA
And we de-bagged all those touts.

DAVY
There's only one way to regulate
anti-social behaviour in the community and that is
through de-beggin' the perpetrators.

BIG SADIE
You see love. The DLA had plenty of successes. More
importantly, you stood up to our Lisburn oppressors and for a
while the community respected you for it. But
somewhere along the line, it lost its way.

DAVY
And now here we are.

TINA
We've no choice Davy, we have to surrender.

DAVY
But we'll go to jail.

HORSE
I'd rather go to jail than be soaked Davy.

BIG SADIE
Horse is right. It'll only be for a few years.

DAVY
And do you think Crystal would wait for me?

BIG SADIE
Of course

DAVY
But do you think she'd feel the same way about me?

HORSE
Are ya mad? After a few years inside, she'd be busting her balls to see you!

*They square up again.*

*Big Sadie releases another squirt in the air.*

BIG SADIE
Children. Wise up. You need a good boot in the hole the pair of you.

TINA
She's right lads.

BIG SADIE
Enough. Now I've been stuck in this bank since 7 o'clock this mornin'. I only volunteer you know. I don't get a light out of this place. I do it because I'm a position where I can just about afford to help those less fortunate. The volunteer workers, the people who raise money for charity, the carers and the people who have had to pack in their jobs to look after others - they're the real protectors of the community. So stop behaving like a couple of school boys and face the consequences of your actions today.

DAVY
You think you have us sussed. Don't you? Well things weren't rosey for people like us growing up either. Horse's family were absolutely skint.

HORSE
It's true. My da was so poor, he had to do his first drive-by shooting using the 4a bus.

DAVY
And Tina. She lived in a right shit hole.

TINA
Aye, my ma left the chip pan on and the house burnt down. The insurance surveyor said the fire caused 15 grand's worth of improvements.

DAVY
I remember we went on a school trip to the duck pond in Ards. We were that skinny the ducks used to throw bread at us.

BIG SADIE
That is awful son.

DAVY
There used to be joke in our school about my da.

BIG SADIE
What was it?

DAVY
What's the difference between Davy Taylor Snr and a pizza?

BIG SADIE
What?

HORSE
A pizza can feed a family of four

*Horse laughs hysterically.*

HORSE
Ah it still gets me.

BIG SADIE
Ok, fair enough. Maybe you all had it tough growing up.
But that doesn't give you a blank cheque to behave
whatever way you want for the rest of your days.

DAVY
I'm not making exuses. I just want you to know why I
was ... sworn into the DLA..

*Music: 'Born in the USA' by Bruce Springsteen*

Born and bred in this little town
But it was run by a bunch of clowns
Went to school to learn to read and write
But I couldn't, I was thick as shite, so I was...
Sworn into the DLA
I was sworn into the DLA
I was sworn into the DLA
Sworn into the DLA
Got a few quid and a decent tan
They put a water pistol in my hand
Sent me off to a foreign land
To go and soak a Lisburn man, cos I was...
Sworn into the DLA
I was sworn into the DLA
I was sworn into the DLA
I was sworn into the DLA
Sworn into the DLA
Bought a home up at Dunlady
It had a drive-way and Sky TV

We shook down our own communities
Forgot about making Dundonald free
We stopped being soldiers, started being thugs
We stopped buyin' arms, started selling jugs
I had a night out on the Aftershock
I ended up with a dancer from Bangkok
The drink was flowing I was totally blocked
I dropped the hand and felt a balls & cock
Now I love her I wanna shout it out loud
But I know I can't because I'm not allowed, cos I
was...
Sworn into the DLA
I was sworn into the DLA
Sworn into the DLA
Sworn into the DLA
I'm a single daddy in the DLA
Sworn into the DLA
Sworn into the DLA
Sworn into the DLA
I'm a lady boy lover in the DLA.


BIG SADIE
So where do we go from here boys?


TINA
We've taken it as far as we can go. I'm ready to
surrender.


HORSE
The same here. I'd be happy enough to go to prison now
for a change of scenery. Feels like I've been here for
a month.


BIG SADIE
What about you Davy? Are you ready to give it up?


DAVY
I'll shall put down my arms and surrender myself to the
authorities. But I shall do so whilst belting out the
Dundonald national anthem and then I will declare

myself a political prisoner.

TINA
I thought you said it was all a load of ballix?

DAVY
I have but there's no fuckin' way I'm going into a cell
without an Xbox and 50 inch plasma.

HORSE
I might do my exams again.

DAVY
Wise up Horse. You couldn't even spell GCSE.

BIG SADIE
In some sort of weird way, I think I'm going to miss
you dickheads.

TINA
You must have Stockholm Syndrome.

HORSE
Aye, to be fair now, I thought she was a wee bit slow from the
start.

BIG SADIE
Maybe we could all meet up for a pint when you get out?
You should take me to your pub.

TINA
The Moat Inn?

DAVY
You don't wanna go drinking in there.

BIG SADIE
Is it rough?

HORSE
I got into a bar fight in there one night and somebody
hit me with a stool.

BIG SADIE
That's disgusting son.

HORSE
I know. It was the first time anyone had ever thrown
shite at me.

*Davy leans over the roof top.*

DAVY
Right Officer Good-one, we're coming out, unarmed.

*Davy, Horse, Tina and Sadie embrace.*

DAVY
Right lads. Hands on hearts. Out we go.
God save aul Ballybeen
Ice Bowl and futball teams
And our Shebeens
The DLA set us free
From Lisburn tyranny
Have ya got any fegs on ye?
Dundonald's free!

NEWS REPORTER
Wow! Just wow. In all my years of being an insincere
and nosey bastard, I mean journalist, I have never
witnessed such an emotive event as this one.
Regardless of the outcome today, I'm sure we can all
admit that we've learnt a thing or two about life, love
and the unwavering determination to avoid employment
-    whatever the costs!

The End

# ABOUT THE AUTHOR

2016 saw the emergence of Stephen G Large as one of Northern Ireland's hottest new comedy writers. Founder of and sole contributor to the satirical Facebook page 'Dundonald Liberation Army', Stephen has amassed tens of thousands of online followers in the year since its inception. The 35-year-old's self-published book of the same title stormed to the top of Amazon Kindle Download Charts within a week of its release in March of last year. Stephen was then invited by BBC NI Comedy to contribute towards their 'Tight Shorts' project, which followed the fortunes of both Irish football sides during 2016's European Championships. The sketches he wrote racked up over 3.5 million views online. Following this success, the BBC invited Stephen to write for The Shane Todd Show on Radio Ulster as well as the second TV series of BBC Late Licence during the autumn. 'Carol's Crissmus' was Stephen's debut comedy play and his first collaboration with the Brassneck Theatre Company. I embarked upon a successful run last December and brought Stephen to the attention of larger venues throughout the country. He was then commissioned by Martin Lynch's GBL Production company to write two further plays, one of which is scheduled for a near three-week run in the Waterfront Hall in October this year. Stephen wrote several more sketches for BBC NI Comedy this year on topics ranging from the Assembly Elections to St Patrick's Day. He has recently been commissioned by BBC Radio Ulster to produce a pilot for their upcoming comedy series 'Short Stories for Grown-Ups'. The BBC NI debut of his animated comedy 'Complete Unit' is imminent and has been described as a Northern Irish version of Family Guy. With several other sitcom scripts currently locked in the commissioning processes of various major radio broadcasters and television networks, 2017 could bring further success for the Dundonald man.

Printed in Great Britain
by Amazon